D1406381

Sammy Finds a Home

An Up-Lifting Tale
for Edgy Children

Written by
Otis Russell

Illustrated by
Barbara Harmon

First Edition: February 2021

Book Designer: Wicked Whale Publishing
Illustrator: Barbara Harmon

Library of Congress Cataloging-in-Publication Data
Russell, Otis
Sammy Finds a Home/ by Otis Russell – First Edition.
    Pages: 52
    Summary: When a spunky seagull travels the Cape in search of food, he finds the alphabet as well.

ISBN: 978-0-578-86344-3

PUBLISHED IN THE USA
Cape Cod, Massachusetts

 Long time ago,

But a short walk away,

A colony of herring gulls
Lived by the bay;

They were raucous and loud,
An unsavory crowd,

And they scrambled for left-overs
Day after day.

ut one of their members,

A gull we'll call Sam,

Felt that food could be better
Than 3-day old clams,

Or that stinky old conch he
Found so tough and raunchy,

Or mussels so bloated
They gave Sammy cramps.

rabs were quite good,

But the blue ones had claws,

And a food that bites back
Is a danger because

It can nip at your feet,
Make a lunge for your beak,

And cause all sorts of harm
Before reaching your jaws.

Doughnuts in town

Always came with a price;
All that yelling and screaming

Was not very nice;

And the bits of a muffin
That he managed to stuff in
Were usually covered

With little black flies.

ven dumpsters had lids

That a gull couldn't lift;

He had no way to reach
All those goodies he sniffed;

So the lamb shanks and gravy,
Smelling tasty and savory,

Existed for Sammy

As only a whiff.

ollowing fishing boats

Had seemed like a win,

From three miles away
You could hear the gulls' din.

The crew would be cleaning,
The fish guts careening,

Off the stern,
A buffet filled with gullets and fins.

etting these fish-bits

Took more and more work;

Sam would jostle for leverage
With a shove and a jerk,

Fighting black-backs and terns,
Diving head-long astern,

But these birds of a feather
Drove Sammy berserk.

**H**is job was made harder
Because of the seals

Lurking under the water
And waiting to steal

All that flotsam and jetsam
Before Sam could get some;

It's tough when your meal
Becomes such an ordeal.

Ironically, trying to find fish,
On Cape COD

Proved tougher and tougher
For Sam and his squad.

Fighting birds, seals and sharks
Was no walk in the park,

And he wondered if maybe
His logic was flawed.

Jetting off to the west,
Away from the seas,
One day Sammy chased
An unusual breeze,

And he found a new odor
On an old front-end loader

Outside a blue building
Filled with trash and debris.

Kumquats and kidney beans
Spilled out of sacks,

Melon rinds, turkey bones,
Half-eaten snacks,

Bits of burgers and pop tarts,
Hot dogs and chicken parts,

Sour cream, sour milk,
And a few crackerjacks.

The scenes on this page
Are in black and white verse,
'Cuz we all know that odors
in color smell worse!

iquified veggies

And calcified bacon,

Rotten tomatoes
Just there for the taking;

But the blast of an air-horn
Made him choke on some popcorn,

And gave Sam a bad case
Of shivering and shaking.

**M**oving just down the coast,

Where the water smelled cleaner,

Sam found a large beach
Where the scene seemed serener;

There were folks, foods, and frisbees,
Not a lot there to displease,
Except free-running dogs
Of all different demeanors.

o puppies for Sam,

They can cause indigestion;
His choice to keep flying
He was sure was the best one;

But, though strong and still young, he
Was feeling quite hungry,

And a bird without food
Can become a distressed one.

ver inlets and outlets,

Sammy flew above Chatham,

Fighting all the things nature
Devised to throw at him:

Sun, wind, spray and mosquitos
(He would kill for some Cheetos);

He had to land soon
Before weariness had him.

erhaps all those sailboats

Might mean picnic lunches;

If Sam wanted to eat,
He would have to play hunches;

He'd swoop down, take a look-sie,
Maybe snatch up a cookie;

You gotta take chances
If you're looking for munchies.

uick as a wink

Sammy dove toward a sailboat;

His eagle-eye spied
A blue untended lunch-tote;

But with sails luff and flapping,
Kids yammering and yapping,

He was forced to abandon
His effort to freeload.

**R**ising high on a thermal,

Sam continued his searching,
And spied a tall tent

Having multiple perchings,

And his view from this steeple
Showed him all kinds of people,

Who were eating and dropping...

This gull needed no urging.

Swooping in quickly,

Sammy grabbed - was that lobster?

And the edge of the grass
Hid a seafood kebab; sure,

His options were plentiful;
He had a whole tent full

Of food choices
Better than putrefied oysters.

To his perch Sammy flew

With the spoils in his beak,
But there followed no screaming,
No yelling, no shrieks;

He devoured his plunder
With a feeling of wonder;
Food tastes pretty good
When it's not from last week.

p 'til now, Sammy's eating

Was just as required;

He ate almost anything,
Fresh or expired;

But being able to savor
Such delectable flavors

Made finding more tastes
His most zealous desire.

erandas and patios,

Porches and stoops;
People filling, and spilling,
Their clam-rolls and soups.

With the food so enticing,
On his cake this was icing;
Yes, a real paradising;
He would stay in this nice thing;

It all felt so exciting
That he let go a gratified
Gull-able whoop!

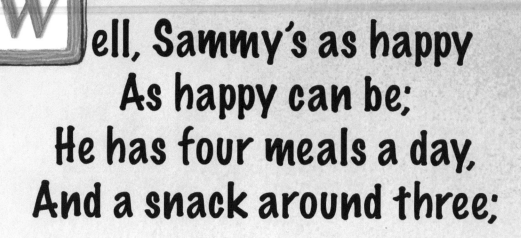

Well, Sammy's as happy
As happy can be;
He has four meals a day,
And a snack around three;

He's soft, plump, and well-fed
On french fries and cornbread;

He loves all he has got,
He's like some kind of mascot;

And it seems he'll have no need
For X,
Y,
And Z!!

ABOUT THE AUTHOR

Otis calls Chatham, Cape Cod home and has had beach sand in his shoes all his life. The past 45 years have been spent in the hospitality business, where he's learned to appreciate people almost as much as sea gulls. Realizing that success in life requires only a great wife, a good friend, and a loyal dog, he conveys special thanks to Monica, Jim, and Luna (knowing an awesome illustrator doesn't hurt either).

Look soon for his next book, The Nor'easter Bunny and Other Cape Cod Cotton-Tales!

ABOUT THE ARTIST

Barbara Harmon is a natural science illustrator who divides her time between Ocala, FL and Orleans, MA. Her training includes a Master's degree in medical illustration, and a Bachelor's degree (double majors in zoology and fine art). Awards, clients and collectors include the National Park Service, U.S. Fish and Wildlife Service, National Oceanic and Atmospheric Administration, Massachusetts Audubon Society, Guild of Natural Science Illustrators, Association of Medical Illustrators, the National Parks Academy for the Arts, and the American Academy of Equine Art.

See her work at www.barbaraharmon.com and www.harmon-murals..com, as well as other portfolio sites.

CPSIA information can be obtained
at www.ICGtesting.com
Printed in the USA
BVHW020850190122
626619BV00006B/292